Zoo Babies

By Richard Vaughan
Illustrated by Jack Whitney

ScottForesman

A Division of HarperCollins*Publishers*

This zoo baby rides on a back.

This zoo baby rides on a belly.

This zoo baby rides in a mouth.

4

This zoo baby rides in a pouch.

This zoo baby rides on the wind.

This zoo baby rides on the waves.

But this zoo baby walks
all the way home.